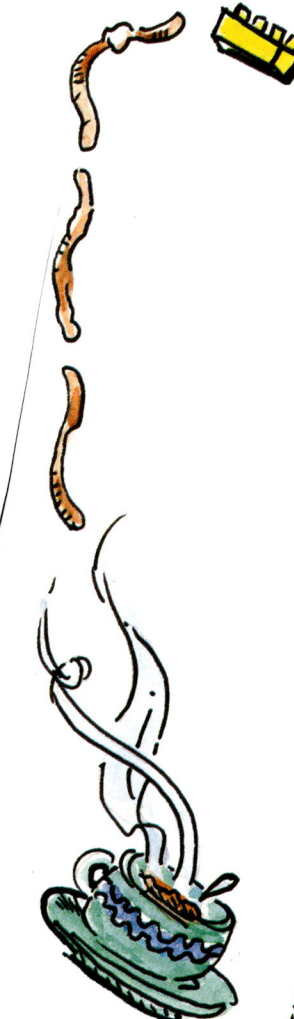

Building Brick
and Other Poems

Contents

Water	2
The Vacuum	4
Wiggling Worm	6
Steam	8
Robot	10
My Model	12
Building Bricks	14

Collected by Brian Moses
Illustrated by Tom Price

Collins *Educational*
An imprint of HarperCollins*Publishers*

Water

I run down hills
And fall from the sky.
I rest in puddles
Before they dry.

I mix with salt
To make the sea.
I bubble and boil
To brew your tea.

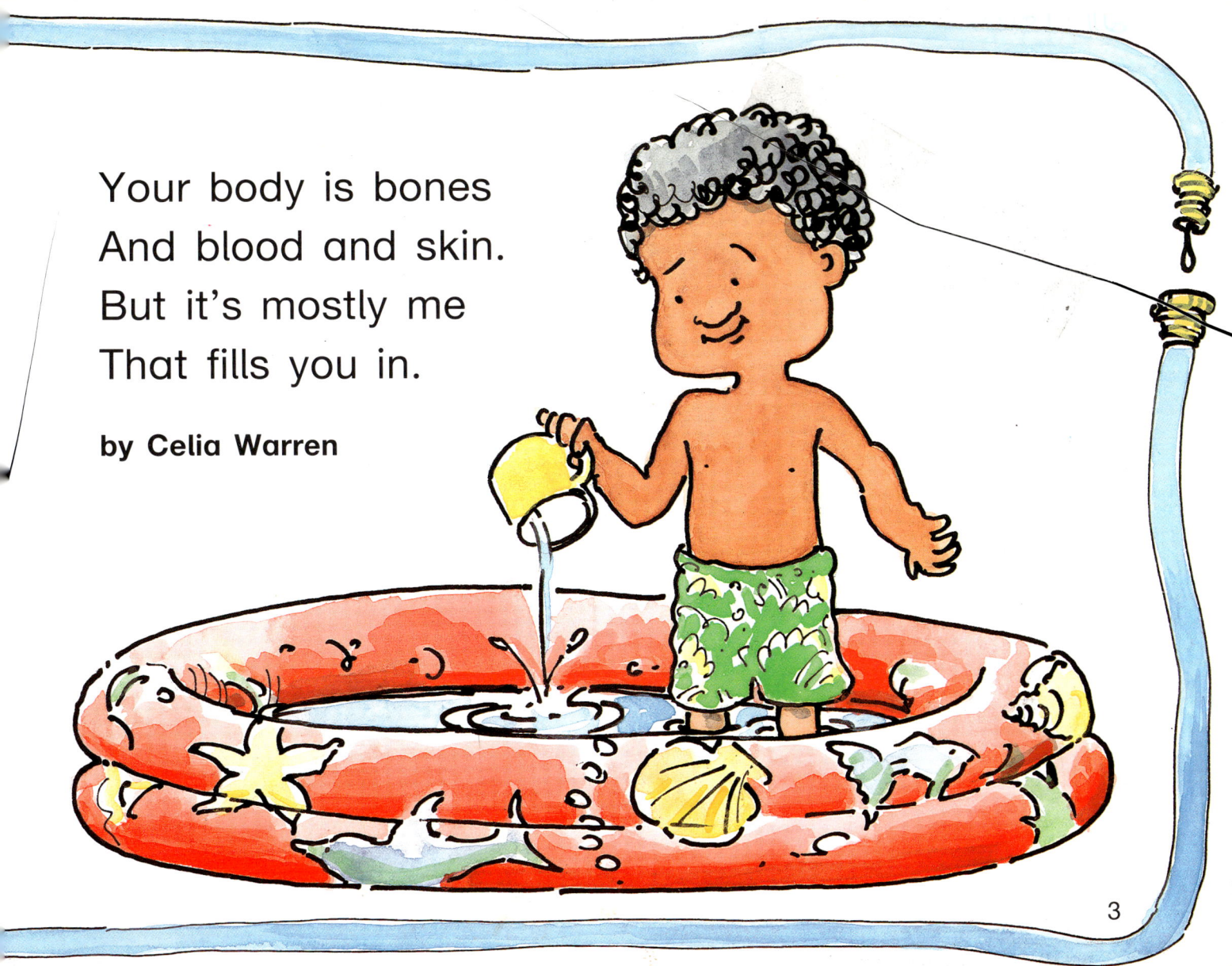

Your body is bones
And blood and skin.
But it's mostly me
That fills you in.

by Celia Warren

The Vacuum

The vacuum eats up anything,
Crisp crumbs, wrappers, bits of string.

It grubs around behind the door,
Then snakes its way across the floor,

Gobbling up whatever's there,
Specks of dust, strands of hair.

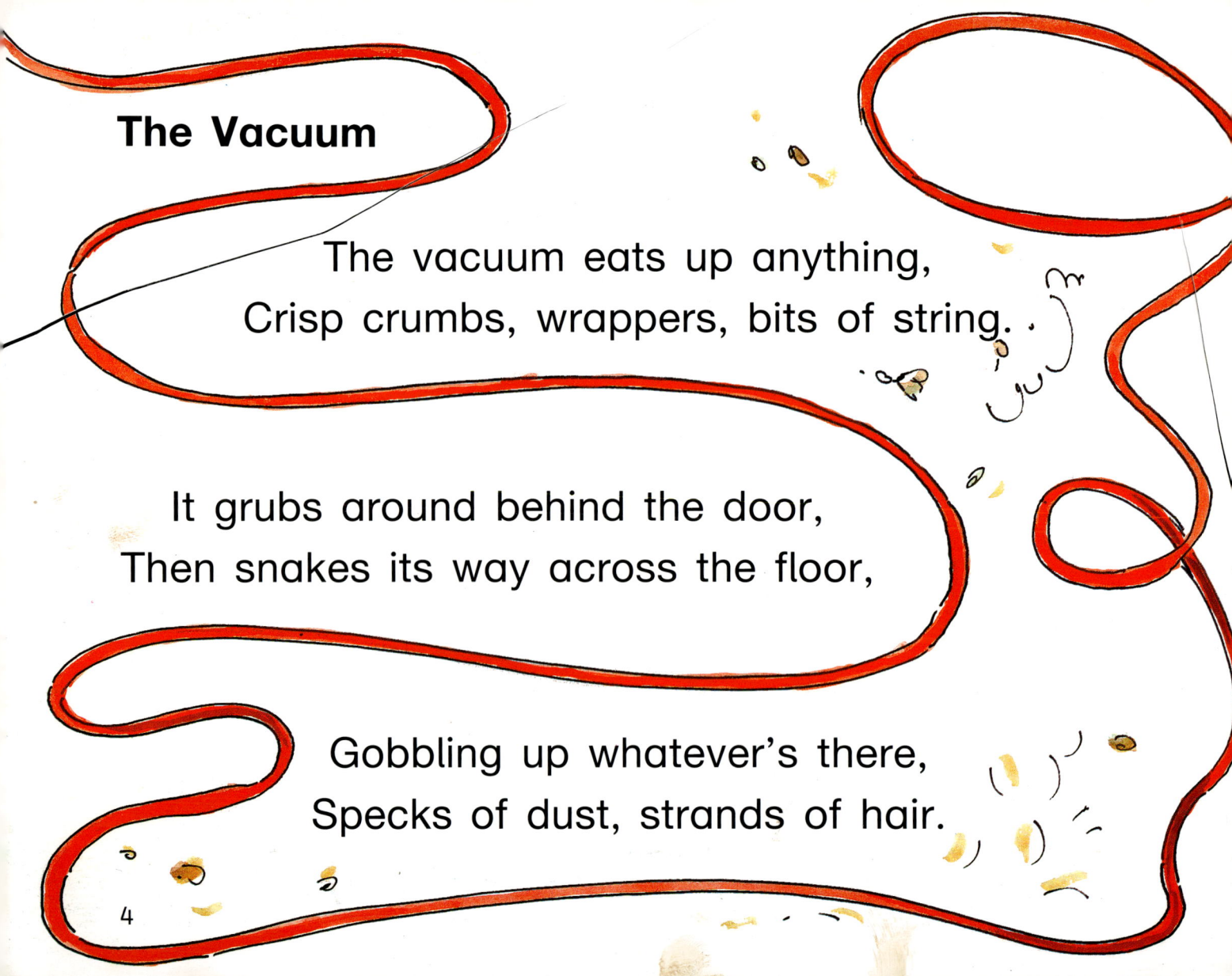

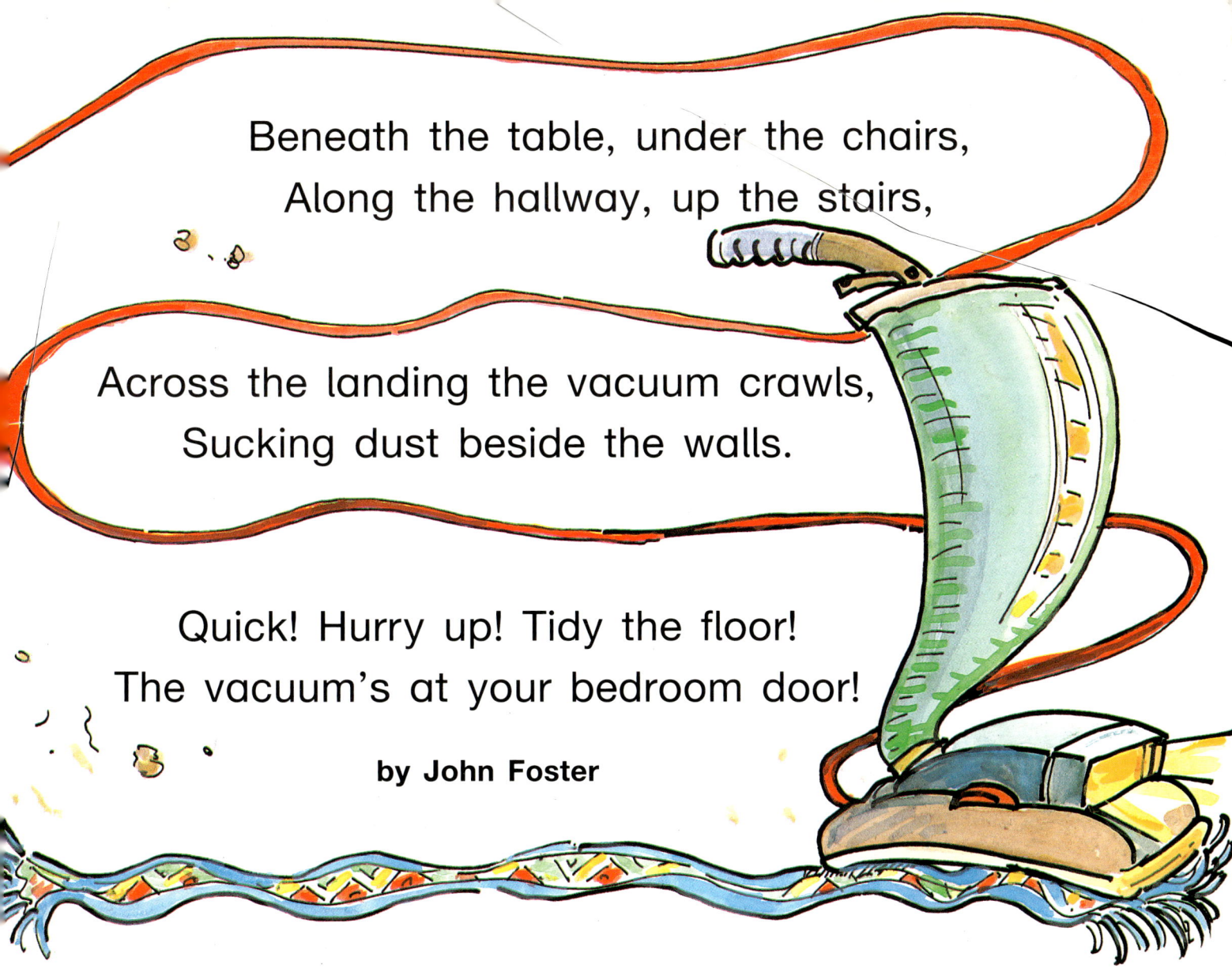

Beneath the table, under the chairs,
Along the hallway, up the stairs,

Across the landing the vacuum crawls,
Sucking dust beside the walls.

Quick! Hurry up! Tidy the floor!
The vacuum's at your bedroom door!

by John Foster

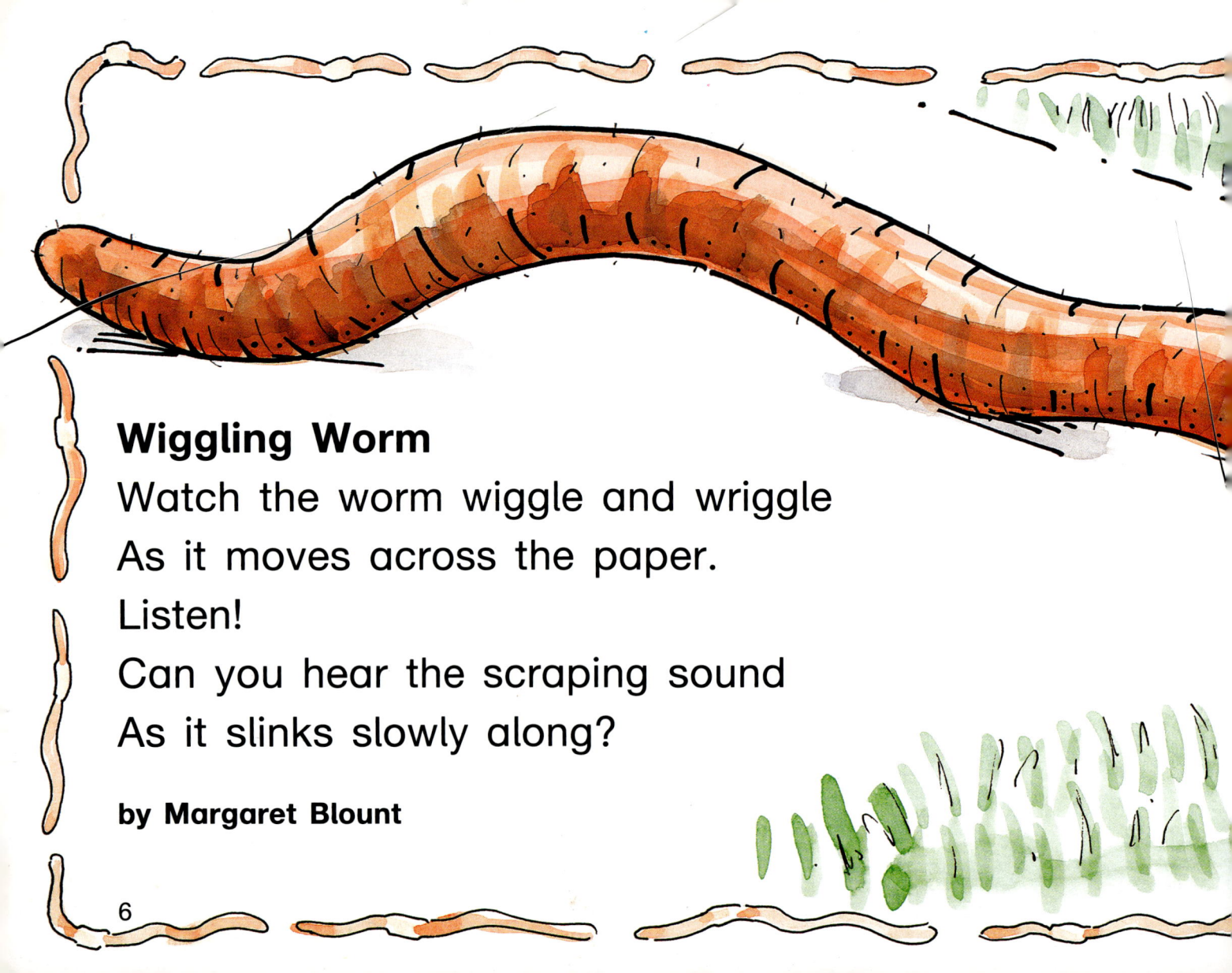

Wiggling Worm

Watch the worm wiggle and wriggle
As it moves across the paper.
Listen!
Can you hear the scraping sound
As it slinks slowly along?

by Margaret Blount

Steam

When I sit
and sip my tea
I see the steam
rise from the cup.
It makes a thin
and wispy stream
that mists and clouds
my glasses up.

by Tony Mitton

Robot

I've got circuits that speak
And elbows that squeak.
I've got lips that can send
Metal kisses to friends.

I've got lasers that look
Through the covers of books.
I can think, I can feed
On the power I need.

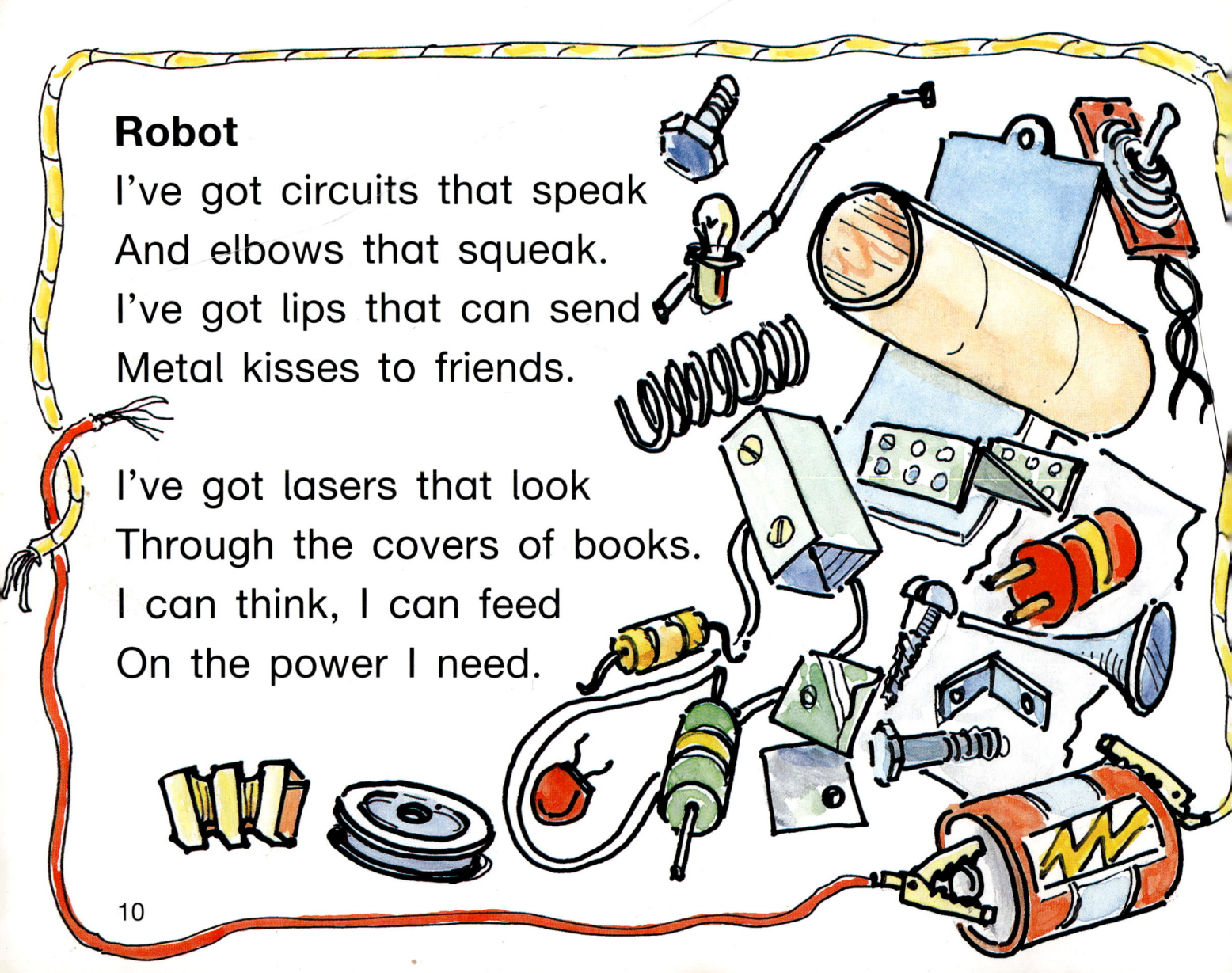

I can stand on one leg,
I can carry an egg
In the clamps of my hands.
I obey your commands.

by John Berry

My Model

A cereal box, bits of clocks,
Cotton reels and rubber wheels,

Plastic bags, scraps of rags,
Bits of bricks and lolly sticks,

A wire coil, silver foil,
Cardboard strips and paper clips,

Curtain rings, a rusty spring,
All held together with glue and string.

by Ian Souter

Building Bricks

Pick
then click.
Each brick
should stick!

by Judith Nicholls